Looking for Sea Glass
Patricia Peters

Copyright ©2023 Patricia Peters
Cover image - Copyright ©2023
assert the moral right to be identified as the author and illustrator of this work.

Apart from any fair dealing for the purposes of research or private study or criticsm or review, as permitted under the Copyright Designs and Patents Act 1988, this publication may only be reproduced, stored and transmitted, in any form or by any means, with the prior permission in writing of the publishers, or in the case of reprographic reproduction in accordance with the terms of licence issued by the Copyright Licencing Agency. Enquiries concerning reproduction outside those terms should be sent to the publishers.

Published by:
Ferini Media
27-29 All Saints Road
Pakefield
NR33 0JL

ISBN: 978-0-954-19125-2

Cover Design and typesetting: Will Goodman - Phantasmagraph

Typeset: ITC Cheltenham Pro

Printed by:
Micropress Printers Limited
Fountain Way,
Reydon Business Park,
Reydon, Suffolk
IP18 6SZ

**For my husband
Jean van Stratum
&
Grace, Max, Anna, Tom, Jesse, Tim, Skye.**

Foreword

Poetry is at its best when skill, imagination and integrity have come together in its making. In this collection, Patricia Peters has successfully melded all three of these elements to produce poems that are as vibrant as they are intelligent, as entertaining as they are thought-provoking, as humorous as they are moving. Language and imagery that is consistently rich, evocative and unfailingly inventive is given further substance by the writer's incorporation of her personal experiences of life, described with an observant and unflinching eye. By turns delighting, entertaining and intriguing, this is a collection to which the reader will want to return again and again.

Michael Fox
Writer and photographer

Acknowledgments

*I am very grateful for the encouragement
and excellent suggestions from
Michael Fox and Ivan Whomes.
Also thanks to Will Goodman for
the wonderful design of this anthology*

Index

Introduction
ABOUT POETRY
11 Looking for Sea Glass
12 A Capital Idea
13 Credits for A Capital Idea
14 Confabulation
16 Writing Poetry
THOSE EARLY YEARS
18 Grandfather's House
20 Digger Shag
21 Those Early Years
22 At Seventeen
TWO FOUND POEMS
24 Henry
25 A Question of Honey
SURVIVAL
28 Survival
30 It All Depends
31 Colony Collapse Disorder
32 The Damselfly
33 Hedera Helix on an Oak
34 Goliath Heron
35 The Crow
36 A Murder of Crows
37 The Beast from the East
38 Ravens in the Tower of London
41 A Mischief of Rats
PARENTS
44 And Sing Like Alan
45 Cut Grass
46 You're Not as Good as Your Sister Win
48 Her Favourite

LOCAL PLACES
50 Looking for Sea Glass
52 Pakefield Cliffs
54 Our Visit to Leiston Abbey
55 Gorleston Seafront
56 Friend's Meeting House Pakefield
ARTISTS
58 Instructions to an Artist
59 The Quilter
60 De Spiegel (Van Gogh's mirror)
61 The Hug
62 A Pride of Rainbows
WHAT HAPPENED NEXT
64 What Happened Next
66 Dead Still
68 My Cousin's Story
70 I Wasn't the One
72 Omdat Wij Niet Vergaten
73 A Bypass Ticket Online
MUSING
76 A Mind Full
77 Two Plastic Bottles
78 Is this Meditation?
80 The Life Changing Magic of Tidying
82 Going Dutch Alphabet
83 A Presence
84 George's Big Issue
86 You'll be Sorry
88 For What We are About To Receive
90 A Musical Wonderland
92 I Found my Voice
93 I had a Dream
94 Musing

Introduction

I came late to the joy of writing poetry.
My muse emerged in 2016 as I started attending
Poetry courses. To date more than a dozen.
From all that information, tasks and feedback
Came well over 100 poems.
Some were inspired by recent experiences
Others came from childhood memories
Many a time I stole the stories of others and
Recast them in the present moment.

There are thirteen Found Poems in this collection
Poems in which I use the words, phrases and lines
From other sources.
No not actually stealing
Nor plagiarising; an ugly word
Sounds more like the plague

There are three Shape Poems or Calligrams in the collection
These have been written to reflect the shape of
The subject being described.
'A Question of Honey' is shaped like a tree.
'The Beast from The East' like a swirl of Wind.
'My Cousin's Story' the shape of Grenfell Tower.
She was an onlooker the night of the Fire.
The first half of the poem has twenty four lines,
one for each floor.

I enjoy reading poetry
Not everything appeals.
Sometimes I don't understand
Some constructions remain meaningless
even after many rereads
foreign words on a lifeless page.
It's irritating. Why don't I understand
these highly praised poems?
I hope that you will enjoy and appreciate
At least some of my poems and
Feel inspired to write a collection of your own.

ABOUT POETRY

Looking for Sea Glass *(Searching for a title)*

Looking for sea glass along the beach is like looking
for the right word to complete your poem.
If you try too hard you can easily miss a rare piece
of dark blue glass, which could have been
in the sea for one hundred years
perhaps it once contained poison
and came from a pirate ship wreck.
Stop straining.
Allow your focus on the pebbles to diminish.
Commune with the sea.
Look at the eroding cliffs.
Read your poem out loud, again and again
Trust your word store
The right word will bubble up from deep inside you
and a rare piece of dark blue sea glass will complete
your poem.

A Capital Idea *(a found poem)*

In my scrap book of favourite poems
This is the night mail crossing the border
Created more than five years ago
If I should die, think only this of me
Before I started my first poetry course
Cocking tails and pricking whiskers
The first word of each new line
Begins with a capital letter
Fair daffodils, I weep to see
You haste away so soon
It was not a rule
The loveliest of trees, the cherry now
More a convention
Making clear the difference between prose and poetry
If you can keep your head when all about you
Are losing theirs and blaming it on you
However, in the second half of the twentieth century
Many poets abandoned that custom
When icicles hang by the wall
Several of my own poems
Liked the capital idea
Hail poetry, thou heaven-born maid
Others found
Stop all the clocks, cut off the telephone
The initial small letters more fitting
Oh to be in England
Now that April's here
They liked the modest appearance
I must remember to be consistent
To thy own self be true
There's so much to be found in Poetry
All's well that ends well.

Credits for 'A Capital Idea'

This is the night mail crossing the border:
'Night Mail' by W.H.Auden
If I should die, think only this of me
'The Soldier' by Robert Brooke
Cocking tails and pricking whiskers:
'The Pied Piper of Hamelin' by Robert Browning
Fair daffodils, I weep to see You haste away so soon:
'To Daffodils' by Robert Herrick
The loveliest of trees, the cherry now:
'Loveliest of Trees' by A.E.Houseman
If you can keep your head when all about you
Are losing theirs and blaming it on you:
'If' by Rudyard Kipling
When icicles hang by the wall:
'The Seasons' by William Shakespeare
Hail poetry, thou heaven-born maid:
'The Pirates of Penzance' libretto by W.S.Gilbert
Stop all the clocks, cut off the telephone:
'Funeral Blues' by W.H.Auden
Oh to be in England Now that April's here: '
'Home Thoughts from Abroad' by Robert Browning
To thy own self be true:
'Hamlet' by William Shakespeare
All's well that ends well:
'All's Well That Ends Well' by William Shakespeare

Confabulation *(a found poem)*

My Found Poem
No, 'twas never lost
Nor did I discover it
Screwed up, discarded under a poet's chair
Neither in an unread poetry book
My grandfather's good attendance prize 1885

A Found Poem, a proper term
Used in those very proper poetry circles, it's
A new poem, using actual words
Written by another
Someone else's lines, someone else's creation
Someone's research, someone's baby

No, not actually stealing
Not really
Nor plagiarising, an ugly word
Sounds like the plague
Was that a virus too?
The rats got the blame
Rats, they fought the dogs and killed the cats
And bit the babies in their cradles.
Not now, Mr Browning, not here.

A Found Poem is more recycling than theft
Reframing, giving new meaning, new life
Sometimes celebrating, sometimes ridiculing
'If' only Mr Kipling had written
A poem for his daughter.

Poetry, literature , scientific works
Headlines , songs, fact or fiction
Can provide the lines
Even the forbidden cliches can be mined for gems
Diamonds to be set in a new poem
Creating a sound engagement ring...ping!

I found a word in Professor Levitin's book,'Changing Mind'
Confabulation
Not a poetic sounding word
More like a medieval torture
His subsequent explanations
Revolutionised my thinking
Re: Memories,
Memories, light the corners of my mind.
Misty water-coloured memories of the way we were.
Distracted...sorry!
I just hope I'm not repeating myself!

His words gave comfort in tragic times
So I stole some of his knowledge
Created a metaphor, a monologue, a poem.

Cathartic? Certainly
'Confabulate'
Of course I would never do that!

I hope he won't mind?

Writing Poetry *(a found poem)*

Some arrangements of words
are immediately inspirational
others combinations take three or
four readings before an essence emerges, one
which I can understand and adopt as my own.

Other constructions remain meaningless
even after many rereads
foreign words on a lifeless page.

It's irritating. Why don't I understand
these highly praised poems?
There must be something wrong with me.

But from all those peculiar lines
one beautiful idea has shone out.
She wrote,
'I spent the whole day
crying and writing, until
*they became the same.'**

Perhaps I need to cry.

* From 'Miracles' by Brenda Shaughnessy

THOSE EARLY YEARS

Grandfather's house

Late Victorian, high ceilings, decorative mouldings,
Idyllic country scenes in stained glass fan lights.
A freezing front room where I did my homework.
Dark passages, brown lincrusta wall paper,
Ageing carpet, Turkey red
Brass stair rods in need of a polish.
The basement cellar for coke.
An Ideal boiler needing regular riddling.
A strip-wash in the Butler sink.
Weekly tin bath in the scullery,
Granddad first, then Dad, me and
Finally Mum in cool cloudy water.

No heat in the upstairs rooms,
Chilblains in winter and sometimes in spring.
Hot water bottles, then electric blankets.
To bed passing dark uncertain corners,
Cupboards with bottled fruit and wellington boots.
Permanent smoke haze in rooms, on stairs and landings
Players, Senior Service. For grandfather's pipe, Digger Shag.
Five adult smokers and me, the only child.

Top of the house my parents' bedroom
And an attic where roof beams creaked,
Discarded objects made eerie noises.
I was put to bed early. Often frightened,
I would call for my mother two floors below.
She couldn't hear, I was too scared to go downstairs,
Passing cupboards and alcoves, where spirits might be lurking.

For many years I shared my parents' bedroom.
The floor below was occupied by tenants,
A young married couple
Noisy in their love making.
She would call out and he would moan.
Was he hurting her?
I was too frightened to say what I heard.
Pleased that my parents were quiet people.

Digger Shag

I hear him knocking his pipe,
emptying the spent tobacco
into an ash tray,
a present from Southend-on-Sea.

I smell his smoke like
a smouldering carpet,
Digger Shag
once advertised as health giving.

Grandfather was not the only one.
Uncle George with his Brylcreemed hair and
floozy in Forest Gate, smoked Senior Service.
His brother Nat had a silver cigarette case and lighter
for his forty-a-day Players.
My cousin Peter hid his Woodbines in his school bag.
For twenty years I inhaled their smoke
passively, my lungs tarred.

Some developed chest pains, lingering coughs,
became hoarse, died early.
Grandfather smoked till the day he died
aged ninety six.

The stinking carpet has been ripped out,
yellowed net curtains replaced by pristine shutters.
But still the Digger Shag is trapped
Somewhere inside me.

Those Early Years

Hot water bottles, blankets
eiderdowns, cold bedrooms
'a lick and a promise'
in a crazy butler sink

liberty bodices, big knickers
school shoes too big
to allow for growing,
corsets, suspender belts
seamed stockings which laddered

nicotine fingers
fags without filters
menthol cigarettes
smoking permitted
upstairs in the bus

the Queen's coronation
in black and white
a nine inch TV screen
neighbours invited
to share the view

Walthamstow Market
Rossi's ice cream
white bread sandwiches
for five o'clock tea

best treat of all
but not very often
three-penny-worth of chips
and a penny pickle.

At Seventeen

It was dark, but not pitch black
Just the two of us in the back row
We'd skipped lectures
An afternoon at the pictures.

Together with a dozen pensioners
Scattered in seats between us and the front row
Those oldies, sitting alone
No purpose, no mates, no future.

I don't remember the film
Only your kisses, being touched
My insides churning, aching, my arousal.

Those old buggers could never have felt
That way, ever.
They might as
 well have been dead.
We were of course immortal.

Now three score years and ten
have vanished.
You achieved your purpose, 'M.B.E.'
Now you are dead*
Someone else will guard
and honour your ashes
in that distant island.

I'm still alive, but alone.
No purpose, no mates and no future.

*Phidias Soteriou 1941-2020

TWO FOUND POEMS

Henry

Brass, silver, pearl,
Wooden, bone or silk,
Attached or stand alone.
I can't bear to look at them,
Hold them.
Each one is repulsive.
Just thinking about them
Makes me shudder and feel sick.
The worst are those unattached,
Hiding down sides of chairs
Or forgotten in pockets.
A collection is attached to my uniform
A few are functional
Most are unnecessary, just for show
When I touch one by mistake
My stomach jumps into my mouth
I'd rather be frightened of spiders
Or kiss an ugly-lipped sister,
Than hold one in my hand
Or speak their collective name.
My nightmare, to be buried in
a bath of used ones.
She knows my name is Henry
Like everyone else she uses
that other name.
That unbearable name.
She has finished clearing the ashes
Soon she'll be calling me.
Even her sweet voice turns sour
When she uses that word.

Buttons!
Please can you help me?

Koumpounophobia is the fear of buttons,

A Question of Honey

This tree is very tall today, seems higher than yesterday.
Lots of branches to climb before I reach that honey. Wished ladders grew on trees. Here he comes! Christopher Robin. Always trying to teach me something. Now it's facts about bees! He's telling me that a swarm has a Queen. Workers look after her. Turn nectar into honey. Honey feeds the grubs…Too, too much information… I switch off my ears… I tell him straight. 'I'm not really interested.'   'Pooh, old chap, it's important that you learn facts. Haven't you ever wondered how bees make honey?' 'I says Who cares?' 'Pooh, dear boy, how comes you never ask me sensible questions?' Just to shut him up I says, 'O.K. O.K!   Can you tell me why this tree is taller today than yesterday?' 'Pooh, my friend, that's a ridiculous question.' 'I says, Let's try another. Can you help me improve my technique for gathering honey so I don't have to climb tall trees? It's not the best use of my puff.' He then says, 'I know that there are some man-made hives laden with honey in the bee keeper's garden. But that would be stealing.' I then says to him,   'Christopher Robin, please explain why I would be stealing honey and Mr Bee-keeper is not?' 'Pooh, you're not intelligent enough to understand.' I says 'I don't know this intelligence. But I know that I'm much better at collecting honey than you. You make a fuss when one bee come near.' I says to him, 'Christopher Robin you are my friend, but you will never make a good bear.'
This tree is very tall today, seems higher than yesterday, higher than yesterday

Winnie-the-Pooh stories created by Alan Alexander Milne, English author, 1926

SURVIVAL

Survival

I feel his warm back against my trunk
taking a rag from his long pocket he wipes his face.
If he looked up into my canopy of leaves
he would see my crop of thousands ripening
getting ready to begin their staggered fall.
But he's not interested.

I know it makes sense that only a few
of my youngsters germinate and become saplings
All forests should have room for variety.
Long ago Nature decreed that producing huge numbers
of offspring: seeds, nuts, spores, fruit, acorns, etcetera,
would ensure the survival of countless species.
But he's not interested.

He returns the rag to his pocket
and retrieves a large piece of white chalk
draws a white cross on my trunk.
We all know what this means.
Via our root systems, other trees have forewarned me.

Tomorrow my trunk will be split in two
my upper limbs will be amputated
my lower half will be wrenched out of the soil
severing my contact with my fellow trees
disturbing the flora and fauna around me.
I won't die immediately, but my agony will continue.
A Calvary cross on my trunk would be
a more fitting sign for what is to follow.
But he's not interested.

The forest is being cleared to make way
for crops which grow in a year or less.
I was a mature, adult tree
when his mother was still a child.
For me there is no return.
He's not interested.

I'm appealing to you.
Please plant a replacement sapling
to ensure the survival of my species.
Help our world to replenish
our Natural Capital.
Without green life we will not survive.

But he's not interested

Written for The World Land Trust Charity Postcard Auction 2021 at The Ferini Art Gallery Pakefield

It All Depends

Wind is unreliable
blows hot and cold.

Do-it-yourself is only for the narcissus
Vegetative reproduction is an incestuous affair.

Adventitious roots are really just for clinging
Single cell division is so primitive, Darling
Only for amoeba types and other blobs.

At the start of most food chains
it all depends
on well designed
efficient exchange agents
bees, wasps, hover flies and others, even
a tiny brush in a human hand.

Without this process, animals would perish
it all depends,
We all depend on the pollinators.

Colony Collapse Disorder - The Queen's View

Something is up!
I should know. I'm Queen Bee here
The king pin in this hive.
A bit special, the sole producer
I fill the honeycomb cells with my eggs.

But something is not right
Where is everyone?
My sterile sisters, the workers?
They do the donkey work
They're not here.

I am not concerned about those drones
Who think they're the bees-knees
Only good for one thing. Sperm providers!
Then they pop their clogs when I've got what I want.

But where are my workers?
I don't go out these days. Too much to do here.
Anyway my pollen sacks have shrivelled
My proboscis has become stunted
And my backside too wide for most flowers.

So I'm dependent on the workers for nectar and pollen
To feed me and the brood
Haven't seen them since yesterday
Are they on strike? They wouldn't dare.

Lost their way? Unheard of.
If they don't return soon my babies will perish
Poor things
And me too

The Damselfly

Eggs carefully laid on the underside
of a water lily leaf
duty done, end of her season
the damselfly looked for a place to die.

In defiance of stringent security
she wheedled her way into the Oval Office
flew onto a desk, closed her eyes
wings slightly fluttering, abdomen twitching
a painless death approaching.

Behind the desk a moving mountain
with a straw topping
spied the beautiful damsel
reminiscent of a previous acquaintance
assumed she needed assistance
with sweaty hands went to touch her
startled she flew away, even though
she was dying.

Aggressive when confronted with non-cooperation
sweaty hands turned heavy
began to chase the damsel
with annihilation in mind.

He trumped his desk several times
accidentally hit the button
and that was the end of the world.

Hedera Helix on an Oak Tree

Creepy, your adventitious roots
no better than a common saprophyte
planting yourself at my feet
stealing my water, air and light.

You promised our union would be
symbiotic, evergreen
when all the time you knew
I was deciduous, vulnerable.

Autumn, you took your chance
feigning affection you wound
yourself around my trunk
too heavy for my limbs to bear.

Penetrated, weakened
I succumbed to opportunists, pests
my chlorophyll disintegrated
my mighty identity lost beneath your green cloak.

Now you take advantage
boasting you're self-supporting
over my dead body
you grow up and over me.

Goliath Heron *(a prose poem)*

To keep out intruders we built a high fence around our small garden with its hybrid tea roses and its specimen trees. No weeds. Dainty great tits and yellow hammers come to feed from a small net bag of unsalted peanuts hung in the white Wisteria. Unwelcome are those noisy pigeons and gulls, their droppings foul our crazy paving. The neighbour's pet is met with aggressive shouts and missiles. That bloody Tom cat! Fortunately clumsy honking ducks and geese require a long runway for landing and take off. We protect our stock of goldfish with a closely woven net which covers our raised pond. Slugs are poisoned, spiders stepped upon and worms tossed over the fence. Suddenly the small garden birds vanish leaving the bag of peanuts swinging. A Goliath Heron has landed on our fence, it's the height of a small man, wing span the length of a car. It flaps down to the edge of our raised pond. Garden dust flies up. Balancing there, it's S-shaped neck straightens, head tilts to one side, it's eyeing up our goldfish. It's harpoon beak poised to strike. Too frightened to go into the garden, we hammer on the glass from inside the house. We shout. It turns to view us, blinks, poops, opens its wings and leaves.

The Crow

Sleek slick unruffled feathers,
soft shining in a watery sun.
Coal black, jet black,
a widow's hat on thin shins.
The CROW...disguised as a simple bird,
discreet, deceptive, a carbon copy.

With beady eyes, feet like hands,
a pointed beak and a sharp mind,
From a murder of crows, he has taken temporary leave.
A walnut in his beak, he ponders how to crack this nut.

Smarter than a talking parrot,
sharper than an eagle, wiser than an owl.
Tis said, the most intelligent of all birds.
Feature of a thousand myths,
and one hundred omens, world-wide,
his ancestors have been both revered and feared.

He can use a tool and count,
this clever Count, Black Knight of the sky.
Ingenious, scavenger, seeker, survivor.
He won't die from hunger,
when he can dip down between the cars,
to feast on a squashed carcass on the road.

How could we know that behind that sooty facade,
inside that brilliant brain,
are stored scores of smart strategies?
On how to live long time, big time,
as a coal black, jet black
black, black CROW.

A Murder of Crows

Sisters Carrion, you have both been found guilty.
Guilty of carrying on like common birds.

From the Crows nest at the top of the mighty Pakefield Oak,
you were spied cavorting, like snivelling starlings,
scavenging for crumbs beneath a table at 'Tea by the Sea'.

Crows don't do that… bird-brains!

This behaviour is obviously indicative of some faulty genes
or damaged DNA.
Either could contaminate our blood line and ruin our reputation.

The circle of black hooded judges are unanimous
 …Execution by beaks.
Let the pecking order commence

The Beast from the East

        The beast from the east mocks
      The bright sun and the blue sky.
   Now
  too
cold
to snow.
Now
too
cold
to melt
  the layer of
    white colour-sucking stuff.
     The snowdrops turn grey
       blue drains from the grape hyacinths
        crimson leaves rust
         orange berries
          grow grubby
           small pots sport furry hats
            primroses suffocate.
             Tulip leaves protrude
              like dragons' tails.
               Forsythia horizontal
                branches are emulsioned
               the Buddha has a
               white lap blanket.
               The Beast from the East
              is threatening
               to freeze to death
              four innocent fishes
               prisoners in their barrel pond.
            Already they wear
           their death caps
         of thick snow
      and unbearable ice

Ravens in the Tower of London

Swine Fever struck the Royal Farm.
No suckling pigs for the King's banquet.
What should the butcher do then?
Poor thing!
He could lose his reputation,
His head too!
Poor thing!

In a dream an idea came to him.
Ravens, roast ravens,
Roast ravens from the Tower.
Poor things!
Don't warned his wife.
It would be the end of our nation
If the ravens leave the Tower.

Her pleas ignored, to the Tower he crept.
With a large net he entrapped the birds
Wrung their necks, gutted and plucked them,
One and all.
Poor things!

When the king heard of the Ravens' plight
He ordered the butcher be hung, drawn and quartered.
Poor thing!
Just before the noose was quite tight,
The butcher awoke in a great sweat.

The dream was the Ravens' warning
Sure thing!
We are not pigs, but noble birds
Defenders of this nation.
Everyone heed our warning.

A week later the butcher caught bird flu.
Then before the year's end, he died.
Poor thing!

A Mischief of Rats

1. Rat Reading
For several nights in succession
I travelled along a sewer pipe
beneath the Water Street
entered Books-Books, via a disused mouse hole
there to read a story of
an unnecessary struggle by a group of
large, foolish animals to takeover a farm.
Ham-fisted fools!

It is possible to utilise every aspect
of human corruption and abuse
and still lead an easy life,
providing one is discreet, practically invisible
one can live within a few metres of humans
and they will never know.
Successful, certainly
Just look at our population
We breed like humans.

2. Rat Race,
From 'The Pied Piper of Hamelin'
'And ere three notes the pipe uttered
You heard as if an army muttered
And the muttering grew to a grumbling
And the grumbling grew to a mighty rumbling
And out of the houses the rats came tumbling
Great rats, small rats, lean rats, brawny rats
Brown rats, black rats, grey rats, tawny rats
Grave old plodders, gay young friskers.'*

3. Rat Bag
Black Death or plague 1347
Affliction came from bacterium Yersentia Pestis from fleas
living on shipboard rats which carried
the disease from the Far East to the Mediterranean then to Europe
The disease gave a dark colouring to the skin of victims.

4. Rattus Rattus
Brown rats, bush rats, palm rats
Kangaroo, desert, wood rats, pack rats
Rattus Rattus the very common black rat
Males are bucks, unmated females does
Pregnant or patent females dams
Infants kittens or pups
A group a Mischief of Rats.

Rat Race - Pied Piper of Hamelin by Robert Browning.

PARENTS

And Sing Like Alan

Alan got onto the stage
round, flat face, small eyes and nose
wanted to sing in his own language
no words, just a range of sounds,
Uncharted notes and unchecked volume
his own music bellowed in earnest
his tongue popping out between notes.

To the audience it was
wailing, howling, caterwauling
we were stunned, alarmed, some frightened
hands went over ears
an embarrassment of giggles, tinges of anger
spoiling our afternoon.
Who let him onto the stage?
It shouldn't be allowed!
Someone should do something.
But no one knew what to do.

I didn't know what to do, then
my dad joined Alan on stage
stood next to him,
put his arm around his shoulder
sung silently with him, a spontaneous duet
a harmony so beautiful that I cry in remembering.
Stating my purpose, my mission
words would diminish this example
not even poetry.
I want to be a woman like my father
and sing like Alan.

Cut Grass

Someone is cutting the grass
its fragrance reaches me, before the hum of the mower.

Langford House residential home
lawns, gardens, end-of-the-road.
Trapped inside, the scent of washing powder
perfumed lavatory cleaners
vomit and the sweet putrid smell of death.

Harsh voices of carers
shouts from muddled minds ignored.
In the next room Alice, aged ninety
calls for her mother.
My father's dentures are lost again
I feel between his sheets
damp after a night's sleep.

I rinse the teeth under the hot tap
scald my hand.
Where am I? he asks again.
I fake a smile at the man who was once my dad.
I turn away and leave him in the care of others.

Outside I breathe in the grassy air
the smell of Langford House fades
duty done, for another week.

You're Not as Good as Your Sister Win

When I was a child
You* told me stories of your childhood
Stories now stored as silent movies
snap shots in my mind.
Silent, except for an indelible comparison
and a coconut jingle.

You rarely mentioned your father, my grandfather
nor any of your six brothers.
You recalled sleeping with your mother and Sister Win.
The three of you snuggling together in the chilly marital bed
cold feet, winter chilblains, infectious laughter.

At seven you contracted ringworm.
Your head shaved, you were taunted by other children
I see your cold head.
Grandmother knitted you a skull cap.
Hair grows slowly.

A childhood chore; a farthing
to unpick a worn out suit.
Ginger, Harris Tweed
smelling of Digger Shag.
If by mistake you cut the material
you earned nothing.
From the pieces, a scratchy dress was made.
You learned to do things carefully
to unpick and remake.
Your apprenticeship as a fine needle woman.

At school you were told,
'You're not as good as your sister Win.'
At ninety five you were still telling me this story.
You claimed it damaged your confidence.
Yet you remain the chattiest person I ever met.

Only in the tale of the annual day trip to
Southend-on-Sea was my Grandfather mentioned.
He travelled first class,
Grandma, children and neighbour children
travelled in third.

Much, much later you confided in me
an incident with your father.
Today it would be considered abusive.
Sufficient reason for everlasting anger.
But I never saw either. I listened in silence.

You told me this story in a way that my feelings
for my grandfather remained undamaged.
Perhaps it was the tone in your voice
Some movies refused to be made.

When my grandmother died, you
with husband and small child returned home
to look after your then blind father.
For twenty years you stayed and cared.

'Not as good as your sister Win'?
In all those years Win never visited her father.
You never complained.
Perhaps you understood.
Had she too been touched?

*Margaret Emily Davies 1914-2009

Her Favourite

A new drug out might help people like you
slows up symptoms.
I'm already slow ask your mother
haven't seen her today.
Dad, Mum died five years ago.
Nobody told me.
We did at the time
at the funeral you sang, 'You Are My Sunshine'.
I saw her yesterday
she lives in the room down the corridor,
do you remember my courting days?
Dad, I wasn't born I'm sure they were wonderful
tell me about them.
This drug delays decline.
You can't halt the declining years
She loved my singing
'You are my sunshine, my only sunshine' her favourite song.
Call her in and I'll sing it for her.

You are my sunshine, my only sunshine
His soft tenor voice after dinner, every Sunday
Dad's washing up song.
You make me happy when skies are grey.
One sweetheart, his wife
one job, one child, long life.
You'll never know dear how much I love you.
Do you remember my courting days?
No, Dad I wasn't there
I'm sure they were wonderful
tell me about them.
Please don't take my sunshine away.

'You Are My Sunshine' song by Davis and Price 1939

LOCAL PLACES

Looking for Sea Glass

Pakefield Beach and I am looking for sea glass
white, blue, green or most rare, dark blue.
Walking south towards Kessingland
six kilometres there and back.
Travelling slowly, scrutinising the water's edge.
Scanning the and still-wet sand
rearranged and replenished by
last night's very high tide.
I'm searching for sea glass.

I spot a square slither of slate,
a brown stone like a lumpy potato
then an asymmetrical triangle like
a multilayered brown bread sandwich
a few patterned eggs, striped and mottled
many perfect spheres, white grey and red
peas and golf ball look-a-likes
a flint in the shape of a human brain.
But as yet no glint of sea glass.

Yesterday, on this excursion, I found
seven pieces of white and pale blue glass
three star fish, two jelly fish and
a flint the shape of a horse's head.
The tide has been in and out since then
taking away what I didn't fetch home.

There's a flat round stone for skimming
bouncing, bombing across the waves.
Much boot-sized ancient white flint
easily broken into sharp edge black pieces
essential for tools, weapons and starting fires.
Then the jewels, semiprecious ovals, pinky-white
mini boomerangs and heads of birds in hard rock,

striped and dappled treasures, tiny abstract paintings,
terracotta biscuit bricks for a dolls' tea party.
Amber a plenty, you could give it a shine.
Penny coloured pebbles scattered in a line.
But no sea glass.

I wander along the water's edge for an hour
my concentration, my focus diminished.
I am looking at the crumbling cliffs
I am praying for a better world.
Distracted by my thoughts
I have given up the search, then
just when I am not straining
to find a longed for piece
something is glinting.
Wet stones can masquerade as glass
But no, there nestling between
a gathering of handsome cobble stones
a piece of dark blue sea glass is winking.

Smooth, and warm to touch.
It has undergone a sea change
into something rich and strange.
Persistently tumbled and ground
by water, sand and stones
it has lost it slick shiny surface.
Some pieces take a hundred years to
become frosted, smooth cornered.
In the 1800s poison potions
were stored in dark blue bottles.
Perhaps it came from a shipwreck
or a broken jar of vapour rub.
One rare find amidst millions of beach treasures.

Pakefield Cliffs

A trinity of elements
the sea, the wind, the rain
are eroding Pakefield Cliffs.

Every day we see the erosion.
Metal tubes become exposed,
three rusty pipes, two metres long
protrude from the cliffs like telescopes.
Clumps of long grass hang suspended.
Tufts of Tree Lupin precarious on a sand platform
alive on the cliff top, perish on their way down.
Lime green lichen, lace dead twigs,
bands of pebbles and clay for potters.

Sand continuously trickling,
grains in a giant egg timer.
Brambles on the beach, like barbed wire.
Trees become replanted,
some upside down with their roots in the air.
Vicious ancient rose stems,
remnants of a lost Victorian garden.
Beneath the cliffs a trailer chassis is exposed
the next day it is covered by a landslide.

Cliffs fall apart
hollowed out by the wind.
Cracks fill with rain, become super-saturated
too heavy, they tumble to the beach.
The sea eats away at the base of the cliff
soil lumps fringed with clover
are held half way down in uncertainty.

Scaffolding poles and metal junctions,
remnants of former times unearthed.
Trees hanging by their roots on cliff top
their branches shivering in the wind.
The cliffs are soft, not hard rocks.
Plants hang limply, dead bodies pink and nude
A flock of sparrows twitter in a dead tree.

Wind, rain and the sea
Nature's trinity, forever eroding this land.
We move further and further away
from mainland Europe
Our exit made explicit.

Our Visit to Leiston Abbey

Leiston Abbey, reconstructed in the thirteen hundreds
Stone by stone moved from muddy Minsmere
The years have dismantled much
But some arches, windows and doors remain
Patched up by Tudor bricks, stolen cobbles
Flint stones and crude cement
Ecclesiastical remnants, perpendicular rubble
Grassy floors hiding further secrets

There's a weary map of the site
Difficult to follow
Where is the refectory, the lady chapel
The sacristy, the high altar?
The sign says this was the warming room
Was the infirmary here or somewhere else?
No one on site to explain

You became aware of a presence
A sensation of something touching you
You asked me if I felt the same.
Did you hear those holy fellows going about their chores
In their cells, attending to the sick?
Those early Norbertines.

We were lost in the ruins?
But found an unexpected experience
If we returned would it be the same?
Perhaps those holy fellows could stop
What they were doing and help us find the way.

Gorleston Seafront

I'm sitting on a bench, looking out to sea
A bench dedicated to Donald Hobbs
He died in 2013.
'What more do you need?' the bench asks
In its inscription.

On this September day the the sun is strong
The bench planks are warm
The horizon, a deep blue line dividing the sky from sea.
Just a few folks on the beach.
'What more do you need?'
.
The warm planks bring comfort to my aching back
I have gardened too much and carelessly
Now I feel an arm's embrace
A feeling I have not had for
A long, long time.
When was I last held, enveloped in another's arms?
The longer I sit here, the more it will hurt to drive home.

On this seaside bench
I'm sitting on a lap
An arm around my waist
A warm hand in the small of my back
Loving, healing, comforting.
'What more do you need?'

Friends' Meeting House Pakefield

Too small to be called a hall,
a house in an overgrown garden
where old horizontal slabs
hold faint names of the long dead.

Enter by a weary iron gate,
there's a funeral of a child,
mourners in long black,
bonnets and tall hats.
Tuppence to dig the grave.
The Suffolk clay is still wet.

Old Friends jostle for places in the Meeting House.
I feel their presence as we sit in silence for an hour.
I see their shapes in a packed translucent movie.
Hundreds mingle, overlapping in the spaces above,
floating on the ceiling, squeezing between the living,
spirits, phantoms, dead, untouchable but present.

This Sunday the living pray, meditate or rehearse old hurts,
minds wander off to private and unimportant places,
most close their eyes, a few to sleep.
Knowing spirits look on,
smiling perhaps, shaking their heads in disbelief.
Even though they read our thoughts
they still 'Hold us in the Light'.

And as Quakers they remain passive, silent.

ARTISTS

Instructions to an Artist

Look first at my daughter
And then at my son
Study my grandchildren
Find that family common denominator
That child within me
Then study my face, not for long
Then talk to me, have a proper conversation
See, I look different now
Capture my essence
Head and shoulders are fine
I'm not interested to see my lines
Soft focus only
You may make the whites of my eyes a little whiter
But I want to have kind eyes with a touch of mischief
Proper eyebrows, not the receding ones I now possess
And the pupils should match my blue jumper
Don't go showing how my lipstick bleeds down
The lines around my mouth
Or that my nose is unnecessarily red
Don't change the colour of my grey hair
I look distinguished
Keep my glasses they make me look intellectual
Yes, and I want to look sensual and not too sensible
The quintessential eccentric English woman
Don't show that flabby bit on my ageing neck
Pakefield Beach in the background
But not where the cliffs are crumbling
Oh yes, I want to look like a poet
That's a challenge, Just do your best!

The Quilter

Have you ever noticed
Artists don't look like artists any more?
Most are neat and tidy
Shy and modest
Quiet and ill at ease
About their inner magic
Their creations and their drive
Which keeps them wakeful, working
And so very much alive.

Would you ever guess
That behind that neat facade
That warm and friendly smile
Lives and thrives a quilter
Her head full of new ideas
Her sewing machine, her needles
An extension of her mind?

In her brain a well-sewn department
Q.I. (Quilting Intelligence) the new I.Q.
Another art form for a special gallery
Look closely at the details, the fabrics,
Shapes, the stitches you can barely see.
Then stand back for a bigger picture.
Of the quilter and her creation.

Dedicated to Jean Minns 1945-2022

De Spiegel (Van Gogh's mirror)

See me in the picture. Arles, late '80s.
Strange perspective. Left of the window. Looking down
on wonky bed, orange chairs.
I was cheap.
He painted my reflections,
thirty times. Some with hats, most with beards.
Sad eyes, looking to the side.
Serious. Melancholy.
He talked to me.
He cried.
No one understood.
Sometimes elated.
Mostly sorrowful.
Tried different backgrounds,
new techniques.
Splashes of paint on my glass.
A troubled soul. Some say mad.
Lost and found himself in me.
 His work unsold.
Theo kept him. I gave him his reflections.
'My friend', he said. To me he cried.
That fearful row. Threatened Gauguin with a Razor.
Shouting. Dream shattered.
His left ear lobe. Severed.
A gift for Rachel. Couldn't pay her.
Bloody mess. I got splattered.
He nearly died. I cried.
The wound was dressed. Reflections painted.
One with pipe and one with a bandaged ear
Japanese woodcut background.
One day he moved out. Left our room.
Leaving me…and my reflections.

The Hug

Is it old age that is causing me
To fall so frequently?
The doctors have yet to decide.
But they have sent me some carers
To help with my chores.

Sensing my depression
One asked if I would like a hug.
We held each other tightly
I could feel her kindness, her tenderness.
I had been feeling distraught
My creative energy had left me
I had stopped painting.
Art has always been my passion
My mission, my reason to be.

Then she suggested I tried a doodle.
From that meandering line
My inspiration and confidence returned.
I have been painting sunflowers.
This carer, a former art student herself
Understood just what I needed.
Her love restored my hope
My passion for painting
And reason to live.

Based on Claire Dowson experience

A Pride of Rainbows

A fanfare of rainbows
an ensemble of coloured arches
red-hot rhythms
dancing, flapping, syncopating
rainbows strung between
autumnal trees
orange sharps and yellow flats.
He has gone.

Magical, vibrant, fortissimo
flags, banners, notes of love
we miss you!
Harmonies green, evergreen
rainbow grotto, holy shrine
hushed pilgrims, quiet tears
the silence is singing.
He has gone.

Letters, photos, rainbows
a melody of hearts, flowers and
spent candles.
glorious, gay, hypnotic sounds.
I'm filled with borrowed pride.
A flag from Dutch Lovies
another from Cyprus
A temporary temple.
He lived by this Highgate Square.
George Michael is dead.

WHAT HAPPENED NEXT

What Happened Next

It's usually a quiet and serene place up here
Souls have angelic smiles and talk in whispers
As they move over and make room for newcomers.
Thank goodness the newbies leave their baggage behind
Many arrive here wearing just their pyjamas
Others in the clothes they were wearing when they left
Some come with not a stitch on their backs.
It's been such a busy year
Even the man on the gate has lost his patience a few times.

It's 31st December 2020 and the man on the gate, old Pete
Is hoping for a bit of a breather.
When 'Lo and Behold' a special fellow arrives.
Old Pete is suspicious, has there been a mistake?
He asks himself, as the newbie starts to make jokes.

Then he unrolls the long CV and reads the list of achievements:
'Acts of bravery, outstanding fund raiser, 'Member of The British Empire''
And there's more
'A reliable colleague, a generous and kind neighbour.
A really Good Samaritan.'
The list seems endless
'Did someone mention unconditional love?
Forever giving, a good friend, a fine father, father-in law
and a wonderful, wonderful grandfather.'
Pappou!
'My mistake,' says Saint Peter, as he realises he has misjudged this fellow.
'You live and learn. Even when you live for ever.'

Newbie is fitted with his heavenly uniform
A white floaty gown which he claims is like
'A big girl's blouse.'
And a set of wings
Like those of an Albino Eagle
Which tickle at first.

He starts to laugh
Even in Heaven he sounds like Uncle Tim.
So he scratches himself
Like all Greek policemen do!
And it loosens a little white feather
Which, would you believe?
Floats down into Highgate.
It is found and taken back to number 51
Where it will be treasured forever
Along with lots of happy memories.

Phidias Soteriou 1941-2020

Dead Still

That's me, my face has been deliberately blurred
they do that, but the rest of the picture is clear.
I can see my body beneath crisp hospital sheets
I'm attached to various contraptions
something is filling and emptying my lungs.
They've taken away my hearing aids and my teeth
I try to speak but the words won't come out
I want to spend a penny, I can't get out of bed.
Various medical people move around me
they are covered in layers of plastic
their names on their face coverings:
Amed, Angela, George, Sula.
Sometimes someone holds my hand.
I'm not moving, I'm dead still.

I'm watching the 6 o'clock news
One of my children must have given permission.
I feel embarrassed to be so exposed.
Dead still in a hospital bed.

I've stayed at home for months
all my shopping was delivered.
I didn't go far from home
not like her across the road,
she went to Lands End.
I had a short walk along the cliff path
for some very fresh air.
I haven't seen my grandchildren for a year.
Sometimes I feel lonely, depressed.
More and more people are dying.

Suddenly I'm not in hospital any more
Then out of the blue, there he stands lightly
'Don't worry, It's all over.
Come inside,' he says in angelic voice.
With a smile he opens the gates
just wide enough for me to enter.

My Cousin's Story

The faint smell   of burning rubber,
a dying barbecue,   doused embers?
Had she left the gas on? Muffled sirens
Some poor sod being rushed to A&E.
This partly posh Royal Borough where
mansions neighbour   with Housing
Association lets   and tower blocks
pack people in boxes towards the sky
a phone is ringing.   And ringing.
'For God's sake who's phoning now!'
Hammering. 'Jan, Jan open the door!'
Neighbour's shouting. Fresh smell of
smoke wafting in through the cat flap.
Downstairs, ringing stops. Phone dead
She opens the front door. More sirens
distant voices, now people shouting.
Roaring,   rumbling. An orange tinge
to the night sky above and beyond the
shapes of the council houses opposite.
'The tower on the way to Latimer Road
on fire, police, fire brigade, it's blazing
They're telling   people to stay away.'
You can feel the heat at the end of our
Street. People are trapped. Screaming

The stench of this fire lingered a week
reached nearly to   Shepherds Bush.
The smell stayed up her nose a month
She remained at home that June night
The relentless TV pictures   became
her flashbacks. The council offered
counselling to traumatised residents.
It took a year for her flaming internal
movie to stop repeating and repeating.
And now another   anniversary, the
protracted Enquiry, the neatly covered
charred skeleton still standing, photos
of the dead. Yes, she sees them daily.

On 14 June 2017, a fire broke out in the 24-storey Grenfell Tower block of flats in North Kensington, West London just before 1.00am. it caused 72 deaths. More than 70 others were injured and 223 people escaped.

I Wasn't the One

I didn't get a lump in my neck
but I saw his, suggested seeking advice.
I didn't undergo blood tests, scans
vicious needles in my already tender neck
I only witnessed them.
Watched an apple corer drill
into his backside to extract a sample of bone marrow.
I didn't look away, I saw his pain, but didn't feel it.

I wasn't told that I had a serious illness.
The consultant said patients only remember a tenth.
He didn't notice how the consultant made sure that
I understood and waited while I made notes.

I wasn't attached to a drugs pole, six hours,
every three weeks for six months
as toxic, life saving chemicals dripped into my arm.
But I waited by the pole till he fell asleep
before escaping to the hospital cafe
where I scribbled down ideas for a poem, talked and laughed with
strangers.

No one said to me. It's fashionable to be bald. Been sick?
Keep positive! Keep positive!
It wasn't me who wanted to scream at the cliches of well-wishers
At altered vision, diminishing hearing, memory loss, personality changes.
I didn't feel like giving up. I didn't experience all that other stuff.

But I did have to manage his displaced anger bubbling up from nowhere.
'Get out, go home, take your stuff!'
Later forgotten, as if not said or explained as my fault.
I was expected to be understanding. I wasn't.

I wasn't the one with a new walking stick
who didn't want anyone to visit or phone.
But I was the one who craved face-to-face conversations
needed to exercise my other self.
With sadness I forfeited tending my garden in England,
walking on Pakefield Beach.

Every three weeks he dreaded the boy consultant would say,
'It's not good.'
I wasn't the one who wouldn't use the word CANCER.
I didn't have it, wasn't nearly ruined by its side effects
I had other stuff. Nothing like his, but still stuff.

Temporarily I rewrote my life's purpose.
Several people understood, many misunderstood.
And I had my poetry.

Omdat Wij Niet Vergaten *(Lest We Forget)*

Hester Hes, born 1868. Died Auschwitz 1942
Max Joosten, born 1932
Gassed along with his mother and brothers. Auschwitz 1943
Izaak van Straten, umbrella seller
One of eleven hidden in a hotel basement
Six survived, five shot or deported.

On the pavements before some old Dutch houses
single stones have been replaced by copper plaques
one for each deported person.
She avoids stepping on their heads
 as if those people are still alive
imprisoned below the cobble stones.

Could the Dutch have done more
to safeguard their Jewish neighbours?
Had she been there, would she have risked hiding
the umbrella seller in her attic
or would she have watched as
his blood rained down upon the cobble stones?

Commemorative paving plaques
this German initiated project began ten years ago.
Soon all the uneven cobble stones throughout this city are to be levelled
Will Izaak and seventy other Jewish names then be obliterated?
Is it time to let go and pay attention to now
or kept, lest we forget?
Omdat wij niet vergaten.

A Bypass Ticket Online

Failing sight, loss of hearing,
Sleepless nights, muddled thinking
Pads for leaks, dressings for ulcers
And painful feet which can't be mended.

You don't think about getting old.
It won't happen to you, not yet.
Not yet, and when it does you think
That you will go there gracefully.

With dignity and with all your
Various parts well working.
Good luck my friend. Only a few
Have managed to achieve this goal.

Mostly this old age blunders in
Suddenly and without a warning.
Dragging you and others down to
The valley beside your mountain.

There in the place of no-return
You might linger, even flounder
For an uncomfortable time
Held in suspension by the nurse.

Who states your life has a value
Or a child who persuades you of
Your function in the family.
Or suddenly, your friends need you.

For those not interested in deep valley life
There should be a bypass ticket online.
Allowing them to leave with grace

MUSING

A Mind Full

Find a sitting position that fully embodies your intention to be
present in the moment and practice Mindfulness Meditation.
Allow yourself a sense of dignity.

Uncle John's chair is hard and uncomfortable.
I can visualise him sitting here.

Focusing on your breathing
Bring awareness to the breath moving in and out of the abdomen.

Really, I thought the lungs did the breathing.
Makes my belly look big. I'm not doing that.
I can hear his chronic wheezing
and smell his sour breath.

Notice the in-breath and the out-breath.
From time to time your mind might wander
not a problem, not a mistake.

'There's a breathless hush in the close tonight'.
My dad's favourite poem, 'Play up, play up and play the game'
by Sir Henry Newbolt. Always quoting it to me. Uncle John said I lied.

If ever you find yourself carried away by other thoughts
gently reconnect with the here and now by refocusing on the breath.

He never spoke to me again. Then he died.

Mindfulness meditation.
Remember you are always more than your thoughts.

Yes, but he thought I lied.

Two Plastic Bottles

Two plastic bottles standing near the wall
upstairs on night duty, you take the piss,
warm amber liquid at uneasy times,
on duty attentive, receptive,
the end of the shift, you're both full.

Two piss-takers waiting for the call.
You know he can't help it,
it's all that treatment,
those drips make him pee, frequently.

And if two piss-takers should accidentally fall.
Once on his way down to the closet
he dropped you both at the top
of some steep stairs,
tumbling, acrobatic, but unbreakable
you opened your flat hat lids,
a pungent waterfall cascaded,
down two flights,
the trickling went on for ages,
a large yellow lake formed behind his front door.

You bounced, undamaged, then
you laughed, and laughed, you piss pots
while he paddled through his own pee
not knowing whether to laugh or cry.

Is this Meditation?

Good fortune sent me a guru.
I found him on the internet,
Smooth dark chocolate voice.
Meditation will ease your anxiety and sooth your stress.
Imagine warm sunlight trickling through your body,
Bathing your organs, filling your insides.
Don't worry, if you wander off, that's natural.
Bring the focus back to the breath.
Count to ten
Then count to ten again.

Grass hopper thinking. I'm never with myself in the here and now.
I've lost the task. Stopped counting, sunlight's vanished
ape-like I'm swinging from vine to vine.
Mind travels wildly through time, emotions follow.
Not sure, past or future, but I'm in a gym. A game's in progress.
A beautiful long-limbed basket ball player is rapidly bouncing my heart,
A few centimetres from the floor. Breath quickens. It's shallow.
How can my heart be out there on a wooden floor, yet inside me?
I smell his sweat.

Is the basketball player my meditation guru?
I contrive a swirl of sunlight to encircle my heart.
Warmth grows out from my breast bone to extremities,
Softly at first. A deep involuntary breath fills my lungs with quiet air,
A lightness in my face unlocks my angry jaw,
My tongue settles against the roof of my mouth.
A delicious taste of nothingness.
Heart stops racing and my feeling of anxiety subsides.
I am counting my breaths to ten and imagining
Liquid sunlight filling my toes and higher regions.
My heart pops back into my chest.
I can no longer hear its thumping.
Is this it? Is this meditation?

The Life Changing Magic of Tidying

The Life Changing Magic of Tidying
written by Marie Kondo in 2017.
I followed her instructions,
made separate piles of clothing, paperwork, books,
miscellaneous tat, mementoes, inherited keepsakes.
Extracted photographs from closed albums.
I held each item before me and asked the selection question,
'Does this give me joy?'

'No' items were squashed into charity, library or dump bags.
I washed my hands of joyless stuff,
ejected, eliminated, recycled, incinerated.
A wedding outfit, never worn,
a pair of blister-giving winkle-pickers circa 1966.
Tightly fitting garments and unwanted gifts.
Bundles of noisy love letters lurking in a shoe box.
Bank accounts from 2000, last century utility bills.
Duplicate and rusty kitchen utensils and those I never use.
Hundreds of photographs, poorly taken, destroyed.

Books with forgotten plots and useless facts.
Said goodbye to covers that I will never read, or re-read.
Farewell to 'Mindfulness', 'How to be Happy', 'We all have to Die'.
Away went a Victorian apron, an Edwardian tea cosy.
Ruthless clutter cleansing,

I was obsessed with clearing, scouring
Until three quarters of my possessions had been banished,
leaving cupboards half empty, shelves and hooks nearly bare.
A throw away baptism.
A new me, clean, free, ready to fly
Pristine, born anew.
Lighter now.
A place for everything, tidied for ever.
Now the air inside is fresh. I breathe deeply.
My squashed Muse stretches herself and returns to work.
I have finally put my house in order.

Going Dutch Alphabet

Amsterdam, a very fine city.
Bought some bagels in The Hague.
Cycles, cycles everywhere, be careful where you walk.
Delft China, 'tis said, is over rated.
Eating raw herrings, a slippery challenge.
Freezing water, so good for skating.
Gosh what big skies you've got!
High dykes hold back water, Hans Brinker is a myth.
I confess, I come here often.
Just in time to see the king.
King Willem married Maxima, a beauty.
Lovely cheese and clogs for tourists.
More bicycles than people in this flat land.
Navigators and ancient mariners sailed across the seven seas.
On the right side of the road for traffic.
Poor Van Gogh's paintings didn't sell, until he popped his clogs,
  ...now they sell like hell!
Queuing for museum tickets can be avoided,
  ...it's so easy to shop online.
Rijksmuseum for Old Dutch Masters.
School children go by bike to school, on roads and cycle paths.
The Dutch speak such good English, that's why I feel at home.
Unfortunately tulips from Amsterdam are grown in Israel. Oh no!
Very soon probably we'll need a visa.
Water, water everywhere, the Dutch will show you how to manage.
Xenophobia is a fearful condition.
You've guessed it, I married a Dutchman.
Zaandam, the best windmills in the world.

A Presence

That humble Hindu would probably have been offended by the conspicuous urn containing a small quantity of his ashes, set in the midst of a perfumed rose garden. Was it from here that this presence emanated and lulled us into silence? Your eyes filled with tears, you later described this as sadness. I felt engulfed by a moving gentleness. Spellbound, we viewed the simple bare cell where he had left his old sandals beneath the bed, a low string cot. There was no apparition of this bald man wearing a loin cloth and shawl, no sounds of his voice campaigning for the rights and dignity of all people. Just an overwhelming sensation that there was something, or someone invisible there with us. Now twenty years later we seek words to describe our common experience. We flounder, but strangely we are able to resurrect that feeling from the rose garden in The Aga Khan's Palace in Pune and the tiny room where Ghandi had been interned during the War. And again I feel engulfed by gentleness and you are crying.

George's Big Issue

His torso is like a partially inflated elephant's stomach.
His head far too small for his frame.
Attached four fat flabby limbs, and some bits.
He hasn't seen for many a year,
Except with the aid if a mirror.
His thighs whistle as they rub together.
Unreachable toes are riddled with foot fungus.
Fingers like sausages soaked in water,
And swollen till they almost split.
His skin is folded and pleated,
Encasing acres of adipose tissue.
Between the layers is raw like a red sunset.
Deep in extra skin are irritating spots,
Mini volcanoes filled with custard pus.
They both itch and hurt.
His teeth, a dirty ivory comb
His finger nails have black hallows.
His track suit bottoms have tell-tale stains,
And smell of dog infested pavements.
His colossal crushing backside

Moves like two battling melons.
Thieves have shattered his glasses.
He can't read easily without them.
His polo shirt has canteen medals over his diagonal breasts.
He's a diabetic and sugar craving,
Too heavy to walk more than a few steps.
Life is less painful in his mobility scooter.
In his grease impregnated wallet is a crisp £5 note.
It's Saturday . Time for his usual outing to the High Street.

'Morning George. Your BIG ISSUE?
No, George, I'm not supposed to keep the change.
Bless you George. You are a beautiful man.'

You'll be Sorry

Turn tap to face red dot
water expected to flow forth
a manageable stream, hand-hot temperature
needed to wash away brown tide marks
on my faithful mug, labelled
GO AWAY I'M WRITING.
Scum left after two coffees, three teas and a poem.
Tap knows it's the same procedure as usual
I don't need to understand how he works.
Do I?
But there's a problem
no hot water
only a bumpy ice cold trickle.
Procedure repeated: three times
accompanied by words of encouragement
'Come on Tap!'
I open the cupboard below the sink where
his nether regions are to be found.
A small boiler not yet 6 months old
white bulging belly, like a corpulent fairy
smug, so pleased with himself.
'I'm efficient, modern.

I supply all your hot water needs,
Including water for hot drinks.'
'Really!'
Red light flashing from his navel
a dial; a dial to twiddle.
Experiment by turning it to several new positions
plus not so gentle words of encouragement.
'TAP!!!'
Still no hot water.
a dirty mug
a poem that might have been written.
Where's your guarantee?
I'll call a plumber
then you'll be sorry.
Why did I give away my faithful old kettle?

For What We Are About To Receive

The therapeutic properties of gratitude have recently been discovered.
'For what we are about to receive,
May the Lord make us truly grateful. Amen.'
Ah! Men in white coats and female researchers have discovered that
being grateful is good for your body and soul.
The soul, whose geographical position is yet to be discovered by
our men in white coats and those female researchers.

We lied, back then, in the school dining hall,
when we chanted that prayer.
'For what we are about to receive.'
Because the stew smelt of concentrated urine.
'May the Lord make us truly grateful.'
Tapioca, the next course, looked like a bowl full of vomit.
However, we were truly grateful that we could hold our noses.
Swallow the lumps hard and soft, great and small.

Back then, sixty post-war children
Squeezed into Mrs Lemon's class.
Our teacher as sour as her name.
She rapped our knuckles for talking in class.
Or made us stand for the duration of the lesson.

My mum said that it was that standing
which gave me my big feet.
'You'll never bag a husband
with those plates of meat!'

For these rather large features.
I'm truly not grateful.
For finding pink high-heels for a wedding occasion,
is virtually impossible in this location.
But I'm truly grateful I bought some in Amsterdam
where the Dutch women there are as long-footed as I am.

These shoes I have worn to five separate occasions.
As my mother predicted,
I'm always the bridesmaid and never the bride.
Should I then be 'truly grateful. Amen'?
Yes! No men! Amen!

A Musical Wonderland in a Hospital Chapel

From the seventh floor we drop
down the rabbit hole lift shaft
there's a white rabbit, a counter-tenor
in a white coat and stethoscope.
'He's late, he's late, for a very important date'.

Our descending scale is halted
the brakes screech in a minor key
an operetta of animals in white
dresses joins the descent.
Nurses? no, I think not, more likely
'Seven brides for seven brothers'
perhaps on their way to the 'Tea Party'
Overture and beginners, please.

Now at the base clef ground floor
do you wonder where you are?
Your face is like a blank Dali canvas
something has happened inside your brain
a bleed they tell me, a bleeding bleed
your violin strings are broken.

I hear music, organised sounds
entrancing, enchanting chords.
'Take my hand, you're lost in a wonderland.'
We follow the sounds,
like the Browning rats and children
from 'Hamelin's town In Brunswick
by famous Hanover city'.

There is a chapel in the hospital
an inverted cone, double-house high
with stained glass, inflamed votive candles
no Baroque nonsense here.

A raised organ, a low altar
a cacophony of spirits.
Oh yes, and an alto-woodwind cross
from 'A green hill far away
without a city wall'.

Sitting on a mammoth bible
is the Cheshire Cat
'In fifty different sharps and flats'
a March Hare impresario
is playing a Stravinsky March.
By ear? yes by ear, long and pointed
on a grand grand piano.

The music bounces off the vaulted ceiling
modern acoustically perfect
and reverberates my insides
a sound both so beautiful
a tempo strumming my emotions
dissolving my mock turtle shell

'Bye-offending brine',
spills over my eye lids
I allow it to run down my face
unchecked, and drip drip onto the score.
What is the score now?

A crescendo, a climax
a release, arelief.
Like the doormouse in the teapot
I don't think you saw my stained face
and perhaps you never knew
Alice, a mezzo soprano, swam in her own tears.

I Found My Voice

No, not my conversational voice
The on-the-phone, face-to-face voice
Regularly exercised with friends, family and strangers.

Nor my poetic voice, my locked-down muse
has been ruminating, sulking underground.
Nor my public speaking voice
Honed by years of practice
But, squashed out, squeezed out, locked out
No one has invited her to speak
Friends, Romans and country men. Not now, not here!

My inner voice has been troubled
No opportunity for outward expression
At least I can write down what she's been saying
Her highs, her lows her ups and downs.

No, this is my Singing Voice!
Coming from a separate department in my brain
Encouraged out by a wonderful teacher* and
Her life changing classes, 'Music for Well Being'
'Music for Lung Health'
At The Seagull Theatre, Lowestoft
I have found my voice along with others
Who in sickness and health have found theirs voices too
We sing of friendship, joy, comfort, knowledge, Religion and love **
As we engage our minds, bodies and spirits
In the joy, the unconditional love, the fellowship
We feel for each other when we make music together

For me, the next step, combining all my voices
I sang at the Open-Mic session at the Pavillon Lowestoft
'The Autumn Leaves'***. Now my favourite song.

Helen Hayes
*** World in Six Songs. by Professor Daniel Levitin 2008*
**** Autumn Leaves, Music by Joseph Kosma 1945 French Lyrics by Jacques Prevert*

I Had a Dream *(A Found poem based on 'The Art of Possibility' by Rosamund Stone Zander and Benjamin Zander)*

I had a dream
We have all heard those words
Martin Luther King 1963
Do you remember what followed?
Words about :Equality, opportunity, dignity, privilege
The American Dream
A Speech lasting 17 minutes
King made a difference
Even after his Assassination
His dream continued
What would King be saying now?
Alive he would be 93.
Could you use those memorable words
To make a difference ?
I had a dream

I plan to read this poem
Listen to people who have different views
Not consider them negatively
Be angry that they don't agree with me
View them as racist, elites, even unkind
I plan to show acceptance, understanding, respect and kindness.
Examine my own conclusions.
Instead of telling people what is the right way
I hope to show those qualities which are important to me.
That's my dream.
Having ceased comparing myself with other poets, performers
I've let go of measuring what I do compared with others
I am focussing on my central self
It's a space of possibility, openness, with an uninhibited imagination
Unfetter by concerns about what others think
Where the best bits of me are
It's a great place to be
I have a dream!

Musing

Where are you?
I fear I have upset you
stolen your glory
pirated your words
claimed them as my own
I realise I have been thoughtless
not acknowledging your part
you are the clever one
in this unequal partnership.

I have stood with exaggerated confidence
before friends and audiences performing your work.
I watched their faces
sometimes they smiled
other times they were shocked
but mostly they were impressed.

You are my best friend
I love the way you work.
With you I feel transformed.
When you are with me I feel elated and smart.

I wonder
do you live permanently within me?
Or do you drop by when needed?
Please return, I'm empty without you.
I promise in future to acknowledge you as my inspiration
the creator of what I have claimed as
'All my own work'.
I pray you are not dead
nor disabled.
Dear Muse please return
I want to write just one more poem
before I die.